PLAYING
SOCCER

(Original title:
The World's #1 Best Selling Soccer Book)

by KEN AND STEVE LAITIN

Special Arrow Edition

SCHOLASTIC INC.
New York Toronto London Auckland Sydney

To our grandparents, Jerome and Shirley Laitin
and
Eugene and Miriam Watson,
With thanks for their love and encouragement.

Cover Photo: Mickey Palmer/Focus on Sports

Inside Photos: Dave Graefe, Paul Harris,
John Kagdis, Oto Maxmilian

ISBN 0-590-32156-0

12 11 10 9 8 7 6 5 4 3   8 9/8 0 1 2 3/9

Printed in the U.S.A.   11

PLAYING SOCCER

CONTENTS

PLAYING SOCCER

Soccer is a good sport because it's the kind of game almost anyone can play. Size doesn't matter. Playing soccer can help you in other sports, too. Running and kicking helped us build up our leg muscles for baseball. Jumping and leaping helped us in basketball.

When we first got started in soccer we felt lost. But we soon learned enough to have fun playing the game. And we're still learning and having fun in soccer camps, soccer clinics, team practice, and in games.

When our local soccer team, the Roadrunners, made the California State Championship playoffs, we traveled to San Francisco for a playoff game in the Stanford University Stadium. We also played a game in the Los Angeles Coliseum before a regular professional soccer league game. It was great playing in front of a large crowd of cheering fans.

If you are new to soccer, we wrote this book for you. We want to pass on what we learned so that you will have as much fun—and make as many friends— as we have playing soccer.

Ken and Steve Laitin

THE SOCCER FIELD

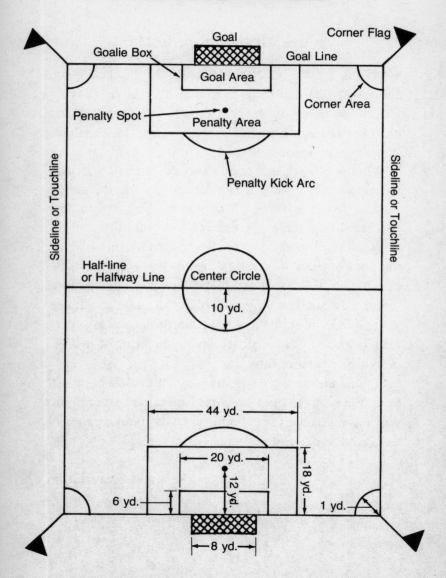

THE GAME

In soccer, the main object is to score in the other team's goal and stop the other team from scoring in your goal. A goal is worth one point, whether it is scored as the result of a play or as the result of a penalty kick. At the end of the game, the team with the most goals wins.

In pro soccer, a game runs for 1½ hours, with two halves. In youth leagues, games run from 40 minutes to 1½ hours, with two halves. During a game, players on one team pass the ball to one another and try to keep the other team from getting the ball. When a team gets close to the goal they are attacking, they shoot the ball at the goal to try to score. To score, the ball has to go between the goalposts and under the crossbar. The entire ball must cross over the goal line.

A player may kick the ball to score, or he may use his head or any part of his body—but he may not use his hands or arms.

There are 22 players on the field at one time—11 on each team. The four main positions on each team are the *forwards, midfielders* (or halfbacks), *defenders* (or fullbacks), and the *goalie* (or goalkeeper).

Each position is located at a different place on the field, but of course players will leave their positions when they need to. Any player on a team can score, but each player has a special job to do.

The main job of the *forwards* is to score goals for their team. The main job of the *midfielders* is to help the forwards score by getting the ball and passing it to them. The main job of the *defenders* is to stop the other team from scoring.

The *goalie* is the last line of defense. His job is to keep the ball from going into the goal when the other team shoots. He is the only player on the field who is allowed to use his hands or arms to catch the ball or block it.

The whole team works together to attack and to defend. When a goalie gets the ball, he starts the attack by kicking the ball, or throwing it, to his defenders or midfielders. They in turn pass the ball until they get it to one of their players who is in position to score.

When the other team gets the ball, the forwards become defenders, too. The forwards, midfielders, and defenders either attack the ball carrier, or cover the possible receivers so they can take the ball away if it is passed. If a defender intercepts the ball, he passes it to his midfielders or forwards, who then start another attack.

It is important to remember that soccer is a team sport. Being on a team means you will be working together with other players. Every player on your team is important.

When your team has the ball, your job is to keep possession of it and move it down the field to score, by passing it to open teammates. When the other team has the ball, you still have a job to do: Help get the ball away from your opponents.

When a player hogs the ball or doesn't pass the ball to an open teammate, he hurts the team. Don't be a ball hog. Pass the ball before you lose it. Dribble the ball forward and pass to an open player. Then run toward the goal to receive a pass. If the ball is loose, go after it. Don't wait for it, because while you're waiting for it, someone from the other team will be running for it.

The more your team plays together, the more you will learn how to work together. It is important for all the players on a team to talk to one another during a game. This helps each player know what the others are going to do. Call for the ball when you're open. It is especially important for the goalie to call for the ball in a loud enough voice so that his defenders know he can handle the situation.

If you know what you want to do on the field, and if you try hard to do it, then you will be on your way to becoming a good player. The more you play, and the more you practice, the more you will develop your skills.

If you want to be a good soccer player, we have four tips for you:

1. At all times know what you want to do in the game. Keep asking yourself: "If the ball comes to me, what will I do with it? If the ball goes to that player on the other team, what will I do?"

2. Be aggressive. Say: "That is my ball, and I'm going to get it and keep it away from the other team." Try to be first on the ball, and two out of three times you will be first.

3. Practice your skills, especially passing and shooting. Start easy and build up.

4. Get in shape and keep in shape. If you and your team are in shape, you'll be able to keep playing longer and you'll score, especially in the last quarter of the game.

POSITIONS ON THE FIELD

Every member of a soccer team plays an assigned position. Different coaches and different books call the various positions by different names. Basically, they are (1) the goalie, (2) the defenders, (3) the midfielders, and (4) the forwards.

1. THE GOALIE

The goalie patrols the penalty area. He is your team's last line of defense. He is the only player who can use his hands within the field of play. When he is in the penalty area, he has that special privilege. When he is outside the penalty area, he is just like any other player.

The goalie's job is to keep the ball from going into the goal when it is shot toward the goal. Whether the ball is in the air or loose on the ground, his job is to get possession of it or hit it where it won't be a danger to his team. He does this by jumping or diving for the ball, or by throwing himself on top of it.

The goalkeeper can see the whole field. He has the best view of the incoming attack. Thus, the goalkeeper has another important job: He gives instructions to the defenders about closing gaps and covering attackers. The goalie also goes out to attacking players when they have broken past all his defenders.

When the goalkeeper gets possession of the ball, he has to put it back into play. To do this, he kicks or throws the ball so that it clears out of the goal area and out of the reach of attacking players.

2. DEFENDERS

Some people call the defenders "fullbacks." Most of the time there will be three or four on a team. If you are a defender, then your job is to stop the other team from shooting at your goal. If they can't shoot at your goal, they can't score. When the other team has the ball, make sure you keep yourself between the ball and your goal. If an opposing player without the ball enters your area, cover him. This means that you stay close enough to him, between him and the ball, so that you stop him from receiving a pass.

If a player on the other team has the ball and is dribbling toward your area, go toward him and stay between him and the goal. Make him kick or dribble to the outside of the field. Practice taking the ball away from a player who dribbles. Learn how to tackle and how to shoulder charge.

If you get the ball, kick it to the outside, away from your goal. If the play is toward a teammate next to you, be prepared to back him up in case he is beaten. Don't let the player on the other team beat you—dribble the ball past you.

Remember: When defending your goal, keep yourself between the ball and your goal. If the ball is loose, charge after it without waiting. Force the player with the ball toward the outside of the field—the wing.

When defending your goal, kick the ball toward the wings. Don't let the player with the ball shoot toward your goal. Back up the other defenders.

3. MIDFIELDERS

There are usually three or four midfielders, or half-backs, on a team. When you play midfielder, you are both a defender and an attacker. Your job is to stop the other team from moving the ball through your area. You also try to start the offense for your team.

When the other team has the ball, your job is either to cover an open opponent or an open area between the ball and your goal. You have to get into position fast when the other team is advancing. You also have to be prepared to back up your other midfielders and your defenders.

When you get the ball, start the offense for your team. Either make short passes to another midfielder or to one of your forwards, or make a long pass to an open forward. As a midfielder, watch for your forwards as they move in and out and around the goal area. Put the ball to a part of the field where they can get it.

Remember: When you play midfielder you are defending and attacking. On defense, cover an area between the ball and your own goal, or cover an opposing player. Always back up your other midfielders and defenders. Always go toward a loose ball without waiting for it. When you have the ball, pass it. Practice your throw-ins. Try to make them long and accurate so they reach the forwards or the other midfielders.

4. FORWARDS

Forwards are expected to score most of the goals. Usually a team will have at least three forwards, but no more than five. Forwards who play toward the outside of the field are often called *wingers*. Wingers take the ball and dribble it toward the outside of the field. Then they either push the ball down the wing, past the other team's defenders to a running teammate, or they cross it toward the center of the field for the other forwards to kick or head into the goal. This cross must be near the goal mouth, but far enough away from the goal to be out of the reach of the goalie.

A forward who plays in the middle of the forward line is called a *striker*. The striker's job is to score goals. Since the play in front of the net is very fast, strikers have to be prepared to shoot immediately and not fiddle around with the ball.

If you are a striker, you should get really good at heading (see p. 28). Learn how to chest the ball and how to kick the ball right away so a defender can't get between you and the goal.

When your team is on defense, most of the forwards should run back toward the halfway line, or even into your own defensive area to help out. You should be close enough to your own midfielders and defenders to receive a pass, but not too close.

THINGS CALLED SKILLS

SHOOTING

Shooting (kicking the ball at the goal) is one of the most important skills in soccer. You have to shoot to score goals, and scoring goals is what makes your team win games. When you shoot, you must shoot accurately so you have a better chance of scoring. Shoot into the corner of the goal, or to where the goalie isn't. The better you shoot, the better chance your team has of winning.

Power kicking at the goal is just about as important as accuracy. If you kick a ball at the goal accurately but with no power, the goalie can save it easily. If you power kick the ball with no accuracy, the goalie won't need to dive to save the ball. You will either kick it right to him, or widely out of bounds. To be a good shooter, you need both power and accuracy.

Practice shooting with a still ball. Then practice shooting while you are dribbling (see p. 51). To shoot while you are dribbling, place your non-kicking foot a little in front of the ball and to the side, so that as the ball rolls ahead it will be in the right position for you to kick it with your other foot.

To develop a strong and accurate kick, find a high solid wall that you can kick against. Place a mark on the wall by taking two pieces of masking tape and forming a cross. Place the ball about 10 feet away from the wall and kick at the cross. Every day try 20 kicks with each foot. When you get accurate, move 15 feet away, then 20 feet, then 25 feet, and so forth.

It is also very important to learn how to kick a bouncing ball. Throw the ball up in the air or against the wall. Run on it and try to hit the target. Remember to shoot the ball while it is on its way down, and not while it is on its way up. If you practice these skills, you will be able to master both passing and shooting.

15 yds.

The Instep Drive

An instep drive is a hard, low shot, usually at the goal. It is called an instep drive because it is a kick that is taken with the instep—the part of your foot that your shoelaces cover. The instep is the hardest part of your foot.

The purpose of the instep drive is to kick the ball hard and low, straight to the target. To do this, your instep must make contact with the center of the ball. If you kick the ball below the center, it will rise. If you kick the side of the ball, it will curve.

To make an instep drive, place your non-kicking foot alongside the ball—about 6 inches away—with your toes pointing to where you want to kick the ball. Bend your kicking leg back from the knee, then quickly and smoothly straighten it to make contact with the ball.

The fuller and faster the knee action on your kicking leg, the faster the ball will go. With your whole leg, follow through in line with the path of the ball. "Follow through" means to kick through the ball as if it wasn't there. Your foot should swing up in front of you until it won't go any higher.

If you are uncomfortable running straight on toward the ball on an instep drive, or if you keep kicking the ground, you can approach the ball from a slight angle. As you arrive at the ball, place your non-kicking foot about 6 inches away from the ball, with your toes

pointing to where you want to kick it. Bend your non-kicking knee a little bit and lean slightly sideways away from the ball. Bend your kicking leg back from the knee. Your knee is over the ball. Swing your leg forward to kick the ball with your instep. As you hit the ball, your foot should be pointing down and slightly outward.

To keep the ball low when you kick an instep drive, lean forward over the ball. Kick with your head in front of the ball, and the knee of your kicking leg directly over the ball. This may sound hard, but you'll get it!

First practice this kick with a still ball. Take a short, unhurried run of about 4 or 5 steps before placing your non-kicking leg alongside the ball. Next practice with a ball rolling toward you from different directions. Finally, practice the instep drive while you're dribbling.

Front Volley

A volley is any kick that is made when the ball is in the air. One kind of volley is the front volley. This is the most straightforward of the volleys. This kick is just like an instep drive, except that it is done while the ball is in the air.

A front volley should be kicked as the ball is dropping, when it is about 8 inches off the ground. To do this, slightly raise your kicking leg at the hip joint. This limits the amount of backswing that your leg has. Let your lower leg hang freely. The kick is made mainly from the knee. Swing from your knee with a short, sharp forward jab. As you kick, lean forward, with the knee of your kicking leg over the ball. Your non-kicking leg should be alongside the ball, with the foot pointing in the direction you want the ball to go.

Once you do all this, you have done a front volley.

Side Volley

The front volley is a kick that is limited to low balls. The side volley will allow you to kick higher balls.

For the side volley your non-kicking leg is about a leg's length away from the ball. Swing your stretched kicking leg sideways, at about a 45-degree angle to the ground. Think of your leg as a baseball bat. Use your instep to hit the ball.

When kicking the side volley, lean away from the

ball. If you are kicking the ball with your right foot, lean toward your left on your left foot. As the ball comes, swing your right leg sideways into it. Of all the soccer kicks, the side volley uses the most leg swing.

When you first try using this kick, only make a short leg swing and concentrate on your knee action. Make a sharp jab from the knee, with a downward chopping motion. Kick downward so you keep the ball low, since you don't want the ball to fly wildly. Chopping down also helps to prevent hitting the ball with the outside of your foot, which would make the ball spin off, away from your target.

As you get good at the side volley, try turning your entire upper body into the ball as you kick it. This will put even more power into the ball, but you shouldn't try to do this until you can volley the ball accurately.

Half Volley

The half volley is a kick made immediately after the ball has bounced and is no more than an inch off the ground. This kick is made with your toes pointing straight down. The ball is hit with the instep. The half volley is a tricky shot to keep low because when you kick it, the ball is already rising.

Place your non-kicking leg alongside the spot where the ball is going to bounce. As the ball bounces, lean forward and kick. Have the knee of your kicking leg over the ball as the kick is made. Swing your leg mostly from your knee, and have only a short follow-through.

To practice all of the volley kicks, have somebody throw the ball to you in the air. Use lots of balls, if you have them, and practice a long time. Take turns. Quickly decide which one of the three volley kicks you will have to use. Concentrate on timing the ball and judging where it will bounce. Knowing where the ball will bounce is essential for a successful volley.

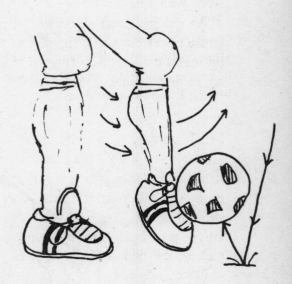

HEADING THE BALL

Heading will let you stop the ball when the other team kicks the ball high to one of their players or when they shoot toward your goal. It also lets you change the direction of the ball and make a quick pass to one of your teammates. You can also head the ball into the goal to score.

Lots of players don't like to head the ball when they should, so it goes past them. If they trap it and bring it down to their feet when they should head it, the other team will often take the ball away from them.

To head the ball, keep your eyes open and your mouth closed and hit the ball with your forehead. Do not let the ball hit you or it will hurt. *You* hit *it!* Have your body and head toward the ball to hit it. Do not head the ball if it is under your waist or you might get kicked by another player.

To practice heading, take a little piece of tape and put it right in the middle of your forehead. Use a light beachball. Throw it up in the air and try to hit the ball with the tape.

As you get better at heading, start moving to harder balls until you reach the regulation-sized soccer ball. Start easy because a bad first experience might make you afraid of heading the ball for a while.

Sometimes we head a tetherball back and forth to practice our heading. Or we hang a ball in a string bag from a tree, and practice jumping up high and heading it.

PASSING

Passing is one of the most important skills in soccer. It's an individual skill as well as a team skill. Passing lets you get past the defense without having to dribble and take the chance of having the ball taken away. Passing can also put you in position to score.

Before you can make a good pass it's important to know where you want the ball to go, and why. And you have to know where to move to receive a pass when another player on your team has the ball. This is called "moving off the ball."

Since getting into position to receive a pass is easier than making an accurate pass, we'll talk about that first. Knowing where you should be when a teammate

has the ball will also help you learn where you should make the pass when *you* have the ball.

When a member of your team has the ball, move to a position that gives him the best angle to pass the ball to you. This means that you don't want an opponent between you and your teammate, because your teammate won't be able to pass to you. If he tries, the opponent can intercept the ball by sticking his foot out or by heading it or by running and beating you to the ball. Move so that when the ball is passed, its path is not close to any opponent.

You also don't want to be too close to your teammate when he has the ball. If you're too close, then passing to you doesn't do any good. The pass won't move the ball very far, and one player from the other team can guard both of you.

Ways of Passing

The most important and most accurate pass is the inside-of-the-foot pass. It is often called the push-pass.

To make the inside-of-the-foot pass, put your non-kicking foot about 4 inches away from the side of the ball. Point your toes in the direction you want the ball to go, and bend your knee a little.

Kick the ball with the large, flat part of the inside of your other foot. This foot acts like a golf club. It points directly out so the inside of the foot is forward.

Raise it off the ground so it is even with the center of the ball. This is to keep the ball on the ground. Now swing your foot forward so it hits the ball in the center, and follow through in a straight line.

You might have trouble with this pass at first, but keep practicing it and soon your pass will be good. To practice this pass, put a target on a wall and try hitting it from about 5 feet out. After you can hit it from there, move back to 10 feet, then to 15 feet.

Practice this drill with a still ball and with a moving ball. Get someone to roll the ball to you from different angles, and try to hit the target. Then have someone roll the ball from behind you. Chase the ball and try to hit the target. Then dribble and try to pass the ball into the target.

Have somebody throw the ball in the air, then you trap (see p. 38) it and push-pass it back to him. Have somebody run down the field even with you, and practice putting passes in front of him so that he doesn't have to stop or run back for the ball.

Passing with the Outside

Another kind of push-pass is the outside-of-the-foot pass. To make this pass, place the foot you are not kicking with about 6 to 10 inches away from the ball. Point the foot out, about 45 degrees from the direction you want to kick the ball.

Kick the ball with the outside edge of your other foot. This foot should be pointing slightly down and in toward your non-kicking foot. Keep your ankle stiff. Raise your kicking foot off the ground so it is even with the center of the ball, and swing with the lower part of your leg. Hit the ball with the edge of your foot, just at the base of your little toe.

Practice the same drills you did for the inside-of-the-foot push-pass. Both of these passes are made for accuracy, so don't worry if you can't kick the ball very far. This is not a power pass.

Now that you have learned the two most important kinds of passes, you can learn how to make harder and trickier passes.

toe pointing
down

Short Chip

The purpose of the short chip is to kick the ball over a defender's head and drop it to your teammate on the other side of the defender.

To make the short chip, place your non-kicking foot to the side and about 6 inches behind the ball. Point your foot to where you want to kick the ball.

Kick the ball with the top, flat part of your foot, where your toes end. Make a downward jab into the ground so your toes slide under the ball. Swing mostly with the lower part of your kicking leg. There is no follow-through for this pass. The ball should rise steeply off the ground, about 6 to 8 feet in the air, and it should have lots of backspin.

To learn the chip, have somebody roll the ball to you. Have your toes on the ground and your heel off. Let the ball roll up your foot. As the ball just gets on your foot, lift your foot in the air about 2 inches. The ball should come up about chest high.

This drill will help you get your foot under the ball. After you practice this, have the ball rolled to you and then make a chip pass. After you get good at that, practice making the chip pass over somebody's head from a still ball, or after dribbling.

Wall Pass

The wall pass is both a pass and a play. It is a quick exchange of passes by which two attacking teammates can move the ball past an opponent. The wall pass is used to get closer to a scoring position. It is called the wall pass because it reminds people of a ball being kicked at an angle against a wall, and then bouncing back again at an angle.

As one attacker approaches the opponent, he passes to his teammate who is next to, but a bit away from, the opponent. Then he runs forward, past the opponent, as his teammate passes the ball back to him. When the wall pass is performed correctly, it can be a very threatening move to the other team.

The pass by the attacker can be an outside- or an inside-of-the-foot pass. The attacker should pass the ball as the opponent starts coming close to him. His teammate then returns the ball with an inside-of-the-foot pass. If possible, he does not trap the ball. This is so the opponent won't have much time to react. He passes the ball to the open space behind the opponent and in front of his teammate.

The attacker should run past the opponent and receive the ball without stopping or breaking his running stride. The ball should be passed so smoothly that the movement of both players and ball appears continuous.

Pacing Passes

When your team is passing, you and your teammates should be moving around looking for open space. When you're running with the ball, your teammates should be running also. When you pass the ball, don't pass it directly to a teammate or the ball will go behind him as he runs, and he won't be able to get it. Pass the ball ahead of your teammate so that he comes to it as he runs. This is called pacing a pass.

You must pass the ball so that your teammate can get possession of the ball and control it, without difficulty and without slowing down.

A good way to practice pacing is to form two teams of about three or four players to play a "keep away" game. In "keep away" each team passes the ball around, trying not to let the other team get possession of it. The first team to complete 5 passes in a row without the other team touching the ball wins. Everyone on your team should be moving around to open space so that they are in position to receive a pass. As soon as you pass the ball, move into open space so you can receive a return pass.

Practice this skill often, and use it in your games. Always remember to move into open space and to pace your passes. You and your teammates should talk to each other so all of you will know when the pass will be made, where the ball is going to be passed, and where the receivers should move to receive a pass.

TRAPPING

Head Trap

Trapping is the way a player brings a ball under control. The head trap is used on falling balls about head high. If there is nobody on your team near you, instead of heading the ball to no one, you can trap it and play the ball yourself. The forehead is used to make this trap. Adjust the angle of your head according to the flight of the ball so the ball hits the middle of your forehead. The steeper the drop, the more your head should be tilted back.

Bend your knees slightly. Place one foot slightly in back of the other, and about shoulders' length apart. Watch the ball all the way to your forehead. As the ball hits, bend your front knee, so your whole body is lowered. This is to cushion the ball so it bounces upward a little, then falls right in front of you.

Practice this trap a lot, because it is difficult to do. You can practice this by yourself by throwing the ball straight up in the air. Also, get a friend to throw the ball so you get practice trapping it at different angles. Practice running to where the ball will drop. Quickly plant yourself, trap it, and run again with the ball at your feet. We think this is the hardest kind of trap in soccer.

Sole-of-the-Foot Trap

The sole-of-the-foot trap can be used to control rolling balls or bouncing balls. To make this trap, the ball is stopped between the bottom of your foot and the ground.

When you use this trap, face the path of the ball and crouch your body slightly.

Your weight is on your non-trapping leg. Place this foot a little to the side of the path the ball is taking, and point it toward the ball. Bend your knee slightly.

Place your trapping leg about a foot in front of you and bend it a little. Point your toes up and raise your heel about 4 inches off the ground. Hold your arms out from your sides a little to help keep your balance.

As the ball comes to you, get ready for the trap. As soon as the sole of your foot and the ball make contact, shift your weight to your trapping leg and wedge the ball between the sole of your foot and the ground. Do this by rotating your foot forward and downward from your ankle so your foot is on the upper half of the ball facing you. Don't put your foot directly on top of the ball because you might lose balance and step over the ball.

Inside-of-the-Foot Trap

To make an inside-of-the-foot trap, face your body toward the ball. Point your non-trapping foot toward the ball so that when it comes it will roll right by the inside of your foot. Turn the inside of your trapping foot toward the ball. Stand so your heels are a couple of inches apart. Lean slightly forward. Raise your trapping leg so it is even with the center of the ball, and bend your knee slightly.

Let the ball hit the inside of your trapping foot between your toes and your ankle. As the ball hits, immediately move your leg back—not up. This cushions the ball so it won't bounce away from you. Keep the inside of your foot turned toward the ball. The harder the ball is kicked to you, the faster and sharper you have to move your leg back.

Another way to help stop a fast-moving ball is to stick your trapping foot in front of your other foot, so you can pull it back even farther for more cushion. But still keep it even with the center of the ball.

Most balls can be stopped with just a light touch with cushioning. They should bounce about 12 inches in front of you so you can make your next move. From this position you can dribble the ball, pass it, or shoot it.

This trap can be made from a rolling ball on the ground or from a ball that is in the air. Remember, you have to get your foot even with the center of the ball. If your foot is too high, the ball will roll under it. If your foot is too low, the ball will bounce over it.

Outside-of-the-Foot Trap

The outside-of-the-foot trap can be used to trap ground balls and bouncing balls. The outside of your foot, between your little toe and your ankle, is used to make this trap.

To trap a ground ball, face the path of the rolling ball. Place your non-trapping foot sideways so your toe is pointing slightly outward and the inside of your foot is facing the ball. Bend your leg a little.

Your trapping foot is off the ground, slightly in front of your other foot. Point your foot in and down from your ankle. Lock your foot in this position. Now the side of your little toe is facing the ball. As the ball rolls to you, get ready and watch it all the way to the trap. As soon as the ball makes contact with your foot, move your leg back slightly, to cushion the ball. Then quickly move it forward to push the ball out in front of you. Now you are ready for your next move.

You trap a bouncing ball right after it bounces. Place your non-trapping foot on the ground with the inside facing the ball. Your trapping foot is pointed down and in, and is locked at the ankle. Lift it over your non-trapping foot and slightly out in front. As soon as the ball bounces, swing your leg across your body and hit the ball with the outside of your foot. The ball should land slightly to the side of you. Now turn toward the ball, and you are ready for your next move.

Chest Trap

The chest trap is probably the second most popular trap in soccer. It is used to control high-kicked or high-bouncing balls.

There are two kinds of chest traps. For both, the middle of your chest, just above your stomach, is used.

To make the chest trap for high balls, you should have your feet even with each other, about shoulders' length apart. Bend your knees and lean slightly back from your waist. As the ball comes toward you, lean a little further back and spread your arms out. This helps stretch your chest, and helps you keep your balance. It also makes sure that you don't handle the ball.

When the ball comes, take a deep breath, and as soon as it hits your chest, let your breath out to get extra cushioning. The ball should bounce off your chest to your feet so you can make your next move.

The other kind of chest trap is for bouncing balls or balls coming upward at your chest. For this trap, place your feet even with each other, about shoulders' length apart. Lean slightly forward from your waist. Keep your arms out. When the ball comes toward you, lean forward and put your chest into the ball. This is almost like the motion for heading the ball except you let the ball hit your chest. The ball will fall right in front of you so you're ready for your next move.

When you practice the chest trap, have somebody just toss the ball lightly to you from about 5 feet away. Don't close your eyes. As you get good at this, have them toss the ball from farther back. Then have them start throwing a little harder, then still a little harder. Pretty soon you'll be able to chest trap a ball that has been kicked.

A problem you may develop when you start chest trapping is putting your hands in the way of the ball when it comes. To overcome this habit, hold a small rock or something like that in each hand to remind you not to move your hands in the way of the ball.

Thigh Trap

The thigh trap is used on steeply falling balls. To make a thigh trap, use the flat part of your upper leg. When the ball comes, raise your trapping leg toward the ball. Bend your knee so your lower leg is hanging down.

How high you raise your leg depends on how fast the ball is coming. But never lift your leg above your waist. Relax your muscles. Don't flex them. Bend your non-trapping leg slightly and point your foot forward.

As the ball hits your thigh, draw your leg down to cushion the ball. Your relaxed muscles will help cushion the ball, too. Now the ball should bounce lightly up and then drop to the ground.

If the ball comes to you lower than you expect, just bend the knee of your non-trapping leg a little more and raise your trapping thigh only slightly. As the ball hits your thigh, move your leg back to cushion the ball. This way when the ball hits you, it will bounce slightly forward, instead of bouncing up.

Trapping on the Run

After you have practiced these different kinds of traps in drills, you should try to do them on the run.

When you do these traps on the run, you have to control the ball's forward movement so it will bounce ahead of you and you can keep running. Be careful not to let the ball bounce too far in front of you because then you'll lose it.

As you trap the ball, keep running with as little interruption as possible. If you don't push the ball far enough ahead of you, you will stumble over it and lose control.

How close or how far you let the ball bounce after a trap depends on the situation you are in. If there are no opponents around you, you can let the ball bounce farther out than if an opponent is right on you.

Also, when you are trapping on the run, you will have to decide quickly which trap you will use. It will

depend on where the other team is, where your team is, and what position you are in.

If you are running hard to receive a low ball coming from your left, you may have to trap the ball with the outside of your left foot. But if your weight is already on your left foot, you will have to make the trap with the inside of your right foot.

To practice all these traps, run up and down the field, throwing the ball in the air and trapping it when it comes down. Use all these different ways to trap the ball.

It is even better to have a friend throw the ball for you. Then both of you can run down the field throwing the ball up for each other. After you trap it, pick it up and throw it to your friend. Then he traps it, picks it up, and throws it to you.

If you trap the ball when an opponent is near, chances are he'll take the ball away from you before you get to touch it again. To be able to trap the ball and beat your opponent, you must deceive him—make him go one way, then you go the other.

To do this, as the ball is approaching, move your body quickly in one direction, then suddenly change direction to trap the ball. This may throw your opponent off balance and give you extra time to play the ball, and more space in which to move.

Another way to fake out your opponent is to change your direction and the direction of the ball right after you trap it. As the ball hits the ground after you trap it, turn in one direction, then quickly turn back and hit the ball in the opposite direction. For example, if you want to go right, trap the ball toward your left, then turn and kick the ball to the right.

This is a good move to do when you trap a dropping ball. As the ball is dropping, swing the inside of your leg around the ball to the inside. Then as the ball bounces, trap it to the outside with the outside of the same foot and take off.

These are a few ideas on how to beat your opponent when you trap the ball. Practice doing them with a friend. Have him stand about 6 feet away and throw balls to you. As you trap the ball, have him run in on you and try to get the ball away from you. Do your fakes and he shouldn't get the ball. Practice this a lot. Try making up your own fakes, too.

Ball Juggling

Ball juggling is an excellent way to develop your ability to control the ball and build up your skill in shifting the ball from one part of your body to another, for trapping and passing. Keep in mind that ball juggling can be fun for its own sake, but it isn't a skill that is frequently used in game play. How many times a person can juggle a ball does not tell you how good a player that person is. Ball juggling is a way to help

gain the feeling of the ball, and the ability to control it.

When you ball juggle, compete against yourself. If you can only keep the ball up three or four times, don't get discouraged. Keep at it. Slowly build up the number of times you can juggle.

Vary your practice. One time, practice juggling only with your feet. The next time, only with your thighs, or only with your head. Then mix them. Juggle a few times with your feet, then move the ball up to your thighs, then up to your head. When you get really good at juggling, try using your shoulders. That's a real challenge.

Occasionally, you'll be able to use this skill directly in a game by kicking the ball up to your head to head it, or dropping the ball from your thigh to your foot to kick it. When you do this, you'll probably catch the other team off guard and gain the extra few seconds that will help you advance the ball into scoring position.

DRIBBLING

Dribbling is running with the ball while moving it with your feet. You dribble to move the ball down the field when there are no opponents near you. Also, you can dribble to get past an opponent when there is nobody to pass to.

To dribble, you run with the ball, moving it forward with a lot of little kicks. Keep the ball close to you.

If you kick the ball too hard, it will go too far in front of you and your opponent can kick it away. If you don't kick the ball hard enough, you won't be able to run very fast and you might trip over the ball and lose it.

There are two ways to dribble the ball. You can use either the inside or the outside of your foot. In both these ways you hit the ball just under the center of the ball.

For inside-of-the-foot dribbling, use the side of your big toe. For outside-of-the-foot dribbling, kick with the area at the base of your little toe.

Kick the ball with soft, delicate touches, just hard enough so you can run comfortably and not have to worry about the ball getting away from you.

Practice dribbling in a straight line for about 15 to 20 yards, until you get a running rhythm and you can hit the ball every other stride. As you get better you will begin to run faster.

Then try this: Dribble at a normal pace, then accelerate suddenly, then slow down, then accelerate again. This way you will get used to rapid changes in your own running pace.

When you are dribbling and an opponent starts to charge you, pass the ball to a teammate. But if a teammate isn't around, you may have to dribble around your opponent.

Dribble slowly toward the opponent, then accelerate

around and past him. The sudden changes in your speed will throw the other player off his timing, and you gain a few extra steps and a little extra space for your next move—a shot or a pass.

If you are dribbling fast with an opponent running alongside you, you can put your foot on top of the ball and come to a sudden stop. Your opponent will probably not be expecting this and will run on past you about three steps. Then you can move the ball in a different direction. This will give you more space to pass.

Another way to fake out an opponent is by changing your direction suddenly. If you want to cut to your right, make a feint to your left. Feint by making an exaggerated step to your left. Drop your left shoulder and raise your right arm. Raise your right foot, as though you were going to play the ball to the left. As your opponent moves or leans across to try and stop you, flex your left leg, push your body to the right, and off you go.

Practice this, and you will be able to fake opponents out a lot. You can try this fake using either foot.

When you're dribbling, don't keep your head down looking at the ball. You have to see where your opponents are and if they fall for your fakes. Also, if you are looking down you won't be able to see if anybody on your team is open.

If you are looking up you won't be able to dribble because you won't be able to see the ball.

The best place to look is at the ground in front of you. The farther ahead the better, but it's only better if you can keep control of the ball.

Another important part of dribbling is screening, that is, using your body to shield the ball. If an opponent is at your right trying to get the ball away from you, dribble with your left foot so your body is between him and the ball.

If you practice these skills and fakes, you will become a good dribbler. And as you get better, you can be creative and make up your own fakes, too. But no matter how good a dribbler you are, don't dribble too often or too long.

A player who always dribbles when he gets the ball will soon find himself getting the ball taken away from him because his opponents will be able "to read" him.

When you dribble past one opponent, don't let success tempt you to try to dribble past another, then another. You should always be looking for a teammate to pass to.

TACKLING

Tackling in soccer is simply using your feet to take the ball away from an opposing player. Before you try to steal the ball, you must think to yourself, *The ball is mine — I'm going to get it*. If you think this way, then you have a better chance of getting the ball.

You must not hesitate or back away from the opponent with the ball, or you will probably not get it.

As the dribbler comes toward you, crouch slightly and concentrate on the ball. Don't watch the player because he will try to fake you out. Start to tackle as

soon as he hits the ball during his dribble. This is the time when he has the least control of the ball.

As he touches the ball, take a short step with one foot and plant it. Place the middle of the inside of your other foot securely against the middle of the ball. Put your weight low and forward. This will force the ball out from his feet, and you'll come out with the ball. The one who tackles with his weight lowest is usually the one who gets the ball.

Practice tackling with a friend. Have him dribble the ball, and you stand in front and charge at him. Also practice running from behind him and getting in position to tackle him.

At first when you practice this, do it at half speed so you get the idea. Then get faster and faster until you can do it at a normal pace.

Slide Tackle

The slide tackle is a very difficult tackle to do correctly. It should only be used in an emergency because if you don't get the ball the offensive player will go right by you while you're on the ground. If you're the last defender against the opposing team, the slide tackle is a very dangerous play. Also, don't do this tackle in the penalty area unless it is absolutely necessary. If you commit a foul while sliding, you'll give the opponent a penalty kick.

To make a sliding tackle, you must fall on the ground by sliding on your side. This slide is similar to the one a baseball player makes when sliding into base. As you slide, one foot should hit the ball and force it out from your opponent's feet.

Don't be afraid of hitting the ground. As you approach your opponent with the ball, slide toward him on the outside of your leg. Swing your other leg across to the ball, hitting the ball away with your instep. Bend your arm for balance. Now get up quickly.

Slide tackles take a lot of practice. First practice sliding on soft ground without a ball. Slide lightly at first, then work up your speed and force until you can do it harder. Once you get good at this, practice doing slide tackles with a still ball, then with a ball in front of a rubber cone. As you get better at slide tackling, try and take the ball away from a friend.

Shoulder Charge

The shoulder charge is the only legal way in soccer of purposely making another player lose his balance so that you can get the ball away from him while he's dribbling.

The shoulder charge may be used when you are running alongside, or catching up with, an opponent. When you are running next to your opponent, adjust your stride with his and lean against his shoulder with your shoulder. Your arm must be at your side. Be careful not to elbow your opponent or the referee may call a foul on you for pushing.

When you make your final thrust at your opponent,

Yes   No

your weight comes from your outside foot. Lift your outside foot off the ground. Your inside leg should be bent. Put your weight toward the inside. Throughout this whole move, concentrate on both the ball and the player.

When your opponent is put off balance, you then have to run very fast to recover the ball. Once you have the ball, you may then turn with the ball and start a play. To practice shoulder charging, have a friend dribble the ball and try to take it away from him.

GOALKEEPING

The goalie usually plays within the penalty box (goal area). He is the only player on the field allowed to use his hands and arms to play the ball. But he may use his hands and arms only within the penalty box. The goalie is the last player who can stop the opposing team from scoring. He has to block all the shots that are going under the crossbar and between the uprights. If he doesn't, then it's a goal for the other team.

The goalie may use his hands to catch the ball, or hit the ball away when the other team shoots.

Blocking shots is not the goalie's only job. The goalie also starts offensive plays, and a good goalie inspires his defenders and tells them where to position themselves to prevent the other team from scoring. The goalie must be able to make quick decisions. He has to know where to position himself, whether or not to attempt to take the ball away from an attacker, whether to play the ball or leave it for another player on his team.

Catching the Ball

The most important thing a goalie must be able to do is catch the ball without bobbling it. To be a good goalie, you have to be able to catch the ball cleanly in any situation.

The first thing you must remember is to watch the

ball at all times—follow the ball's flight right up to the moment it is safely caught in your hands.

When you catch the ball, have your hands slightly behind it. This will stop the ball from slipping through your fingers. As you catch the ball, spread your fingers apart. Your thumbs should almost be touching each other. If your hands are too far apart, and if they aren't behind the ball, the ball might go right through your hands and into the goal.

When the ball is coming about head high, place your hands in the path of the ball. Relax your fingers and wrists. As soon as you catch the ball, tighten your fingers so you get a good grip on the ball, but keep your wrists relaxed. This will soften the impact so the ball won't bounce away.

Whenever it's possible, get your body in front of the ball when you catch it. Then, just in case you miss the ball, it will hit your body instead of going into the goal.

If the ball is shot chest high, catch the ball against your chest. As it hits your chest, bring your arms around to catch the ball, so it is held securely against your chest.

When you catch this kind of shot, the safest way to

stand is with your feet planted on the ground about shoulders' width apart. Your knees should be slightly bent.

If the ball is bouncing up at you, lean forward over the ball. When you catch it, bring it into your chest. This will give plenty of body behind the ball in case it takes a bad bounce, or in case you have somewhat misjudged it.

On ground balls, quickly get on one knee to catch the ball. Scoop it up with your hands and bring it to your chest.

If a player dribbles into the penalty box past your defenders, you must come out and grab the ball before he shoots.

Diving Save

If the ball is coming fast to a corner of the goal where you can't reach it easily, you must dive and try to catch it, or deflect it away from the goal.

To dive after the ball, push your body off the ground with the leg nearest the direction of your dive. Your body is facing the ball. Your side is facing the ground. Fling your arms out toward the ball as your feet lift off the ground. Catch the ball with your arms outstretched.

As soon as the ball is caught, bring it in to your chest. The ball and the forearm of your lower arm hit the ground first. At the same time, your other hand pushes the ball firmly down into the ground. As soon as you land, pull the ball into your chest again.

This skill requires lots of practice because it is really hard to do. Start at first without the ball. Take little dives so you get the technique and so you won't hurt yourself hitting the ground. As you get better, increase the distance covered by your dives. Then practice with a ball.

If the ball is too far away for you to catch it and control it, you can use your fist or open hand to punch the ball away. (When you land, use your arms to break your fall.) This may give the other team a corner kick, but at least it isn't a goal.

Getting Rid of the Ball

To put the ball back into play, the goalie is allowed to take only four steps with the ball. To get the ball out the farthest distance, he is allowed to roll the ball out to the edge of the penalty box and kick it from there. Rolling the ball counts as only one step because the goalie isn't considered to have control of it.

When you roll the ball, run right behind it. You must be careful not to let the other team take it away from you. If they start to charge the ball, pick it up. You may roll it again, around the attackers, but you must be very careful.

When you stop rolling the ball, you have only a certain number of steps left. The number of steps you have left depends on how many times you rolled the ball. You should only roll it once or twice.

To throw the ball, hold the ball with your throwing hand slightly underneath it. Draw your arm back and bend your elbow. Your other arm and your planted leg face the target.

Now, as your throwing arm comes forward, your body should start to turn toward your target. As you complete your turn, release the ball about a foot in front of your head. Don't throw the ball above head height.

To kick the ball, hold both hands under the ball with your arms out in front of you about waist high. Your

elbows should be slightly bent. Take a step forward with your non-kicking leg. Swing your kicking foot up toward the ball. Keep your toes pointed. As your foot is swinging upward, move your hands out and let the ball drop. Your instep should hit the ball just as you drop it. The ball should go high and far. It takes a lot of practice to get the timing right, and to get the power for distance and control.

The Angles of Goalkeeping

In order to be a good goalie, you must know how to cut off the angles of the goal when the ball is shot.

How do you cut off the angles? When an attacker takes a shot from the center, the goalie should be in the center of the goal. This gives the other team the least chance to score because the goalie has equal space on each side of the goal to save the ball.

If an attacker takes a shot from a little to the side, the goalie should move a little bit to that side. As goalie, always position yourself so that there is equal

distance on either side of you where the ball can go into the goal. You must practice a lot to get to know where the position is that allows the least possible scoring.

Have a friend or a group of friends keep taking shots at the goal while you try to get in position to save the ball. Do this over and over until knowing where you are supposed to stand, when the ball is shot from a certain place, becomes instinct.

RESTARTS

THE KICK-OFF

At the beginning of a soccer game there is usually a coin toss. The winner gets a choice of kicking off or picking which goal to defend.

The kick-off is the way a team puts the ball into play at the start of each half and after each goal.

On the kick-off, the ball is placed on the half-line in the center of the circle in the middle of the field. Each team must be on the side of the half-line they are defending. If your team is kicking off, then the other team must not only be in their half, they must also be outside the circle.

After kicking, the first kicker may not touch the ball

a second time until it is touched by another player. And the ball must move forward at least the distance of its circumference (about 2 feet) before play can begin.

The best thing to do is kick the ball slightly forward to another forward, who then either passes the ball to an outside forward or back to a midfielder. Then the midfielder can kick the ball upfield or pass it to another player. The other team will probably charge in to try to get the ball away from you, so you must make all these passes quickly.

When the other team kicks off, your forwards should be ready to run in from outside the circle. Before play can start with a kick-off, the referee must blow his whistle. But you can't start to rush until the ball moves the distance of its circumference. As soon as it does, your team should be charging to try to get possession of it.

GOAL KICK

A goal kick is the way of putting the ball into play when it goes out of bounds across the goal line after being touched last by a player from the *attacking* team.

The ball may be placed anywhere inside the goalie box on the side of the field where the ball went out. The ball must leave the penalty area before being touched again, or the goal kick must be taken over.

A defender, or the goalie, can kick the ball upfield, or they can try various other plays. One play is to kick the ball just outside of the penalty box to a teammate who then taps it back to the goalie. Then the goalie picks it up and kicks the ball down the field. A defender should cover the goal while the goalie comes out.

When you try this play, if the other team starts to cover the goalie after the defender kicks the ball, then the player with the ball should dribble it down the side of the field or kick it down the field. If necessary he should kick it out of bounds. The goalie should quickly get back into goal.

While the goal kick is being taken, all of your midfielders should cover the other team's forwards in case of a bad kick. If the kicker kicks the ball upfield, he should kick the ball toward the wings.

CORNER KICK

The corner kick is a special kind of free kick that is given to the attacking team when the *defense* touches the ball last before it goes out of bounds across the goal line. This kick is taken from within a 1-yard arc in the corner of the field closest to the point where the ball went out.

When defending against a corner kick, the goalie should stand on the goal line and about three-fourths of the way back from the post closest to the ball. The reason the goalie stays back is so he can run up on the ball if he needs to. It is much harder to run backward.

One defender should stand against the near post to block the ball from slipping into the goal. Another defender should stand against the far post, so that if the ball is heading into the goal, he can put his body in front of it, then kick it out.

The rest of the defenders and midfielders should cover the other team's forwards and midfielders so they can't shoot. If the ball comes into the middle, the goalie should grab it. If he doesn't, the defenders should kick or head the ball out of the area. When your team gets a corner kick, the defending team will probably line up this same way.

On a corner kick, three attacking forwards should line up in front of the goal—one forward just outside the far corner of the goalie box, one in the middle just outside the goalie box, and the third forward near the other corner of the goalie box. If your team is attacking, your players should move around so that the other team can't easily cover them. Your midfielders should be lined up just inside the penalty box.

The kicker should try to kick the ball in the air toward the edge of the goalie box. Then the forwards can head the ball into the goal. If the ball bounces out, then the midfielders can try to score. If the ball isn't in the air, then the forwards can just kick it.

Another corner-kick play is the "short" corner kick. The attacking team lines up in the same way, but a midfielder (or forward) runs out quickly toward the kicker. The kicker passes the ball to him, then runs behind the midfielder to receive a pass from him. Then the kicker can shoot, dribble and shoot, or center the ball.

If an opponent has the midfielder covered, another player can run toward the kicker for a pass, or the kicker can just kick the ball across the middle toward the goal. He should kick it while the opponents are close to him so there are fewer opponents in the middle of the goal area. Turn corner kicks into goals!

THE THROW-IN

Nearly every soccer player will take a throw-in some-time. Your team gets a throw-in when a player on the other team plays the ball past the touchline and out of bounds. It is taken where the ball goes out. While the rules on throw-ins are a little technical, just remember a few things and you won't have any problems with the referees blowing their whistles and calling you for a foul throw-in.

The first thing to remember is to keep both your feet

behind the touchline and on the ground. Hold the ball with your hands slightly behind it. Put both hands straight up and behind your head. The ball should be touching the back of your neck. Now bring the ball back over your head and release it, all in one motion. When you release the ball depends on how far you want to throw it. Practice throwing the ball different distances. Aim at a teammate's chest or feet until your throw becomes accurate. Both hands should throw the ball with equal force. The ball should not spin sideways.

If both feet are not on or behind the line, or if the ball isn't thrown from directly behind the head, the referee may blow the whistle and give the throw-in to the other team.

You may not throw the ball in to yourself. In other words, when you throw the ball in, it has to be touched by another player either on your team or the other team before you can touch it again.

The throw-in is often an overlooked move in soccer. A throw-in gives your team possession of the ball. You can quickly start an attack on the other team's goal.

If you get the ball real fast and take a throw-in before the other team has a chance to get ready, you have a big advantage. Your team can dribble down to the other team's goal and shoot, or quickly pass the ball to a breaking forward, or kick the ball across the field to the winger who should be wide open to score. When your team is taking a throw-in, your players shouldn't be standing waiting for the ball. They should be moving around trying to get open.

One play is for a player to stand next to the thrower. As the thrower starts to throw the ball, the player runs down the wing. The thrower throws the ball just over the player's head. The ball will bounce in front of him and he has a breakaway.

On this play, you don't have to worry about being offside (see p.110) because on a throw-in no one can be offside until the second player on your team plays the ball.

This is just one example of a throw-in play. Your team can work out other plays, too. If you practice throw-in plays, then a throw-in could be a very good scoring opportunity for your team.

THE FREE KICK

A free kick is another play-making opportunity which can lead to a goal. When do you get a free kick? When an opponent commits a foul or an infraction of the rules.

On a free kick your team gets a chance to kick the ball into play while the other team must stand back.

When the referee calls a free kick, the ball is placed on the spot where the foul was committed. The other team has to stay at least 10 yards away from the ball. They may not charge in until the ball has been kicked and has moved its circumferences.

In a game, when you are given a free kick, and if any of the players on the other team don't get 10 yards away, you may ask the referee to give you your 10 yards. He will then move the players back, but you must now wait for the whistle to start play. There are two different kinds of free kicks: an indirect free kick and a direct free kick.

When the referee blows his whistle and holds one arm up in the air, he is awarding an indirect free kick. An indirect free kick is called for dangerous play, obstructing an opponent, or for too many steps by the goalkeeper.

On an indirect free kick, at least one other player

besides the kicker has to touch the ball before it goes into the goal.

A direct free kick is given on a foul called for striking, kicking, tripping, jumping, charging violently, charging from behind, holding, pushing, or touching the ball with the hands. The referee will blow his whistle and indicate the point where the foul took place. On a direct free kick a player may kick the ball right into the goal and score. The ball doesn't have to be touched by another player first.

Indirect free kicks are different. A good play for an indirect free kick is to have a player stand facing the

goal, with the ball on the ground between his feet. A teammate behind him lightly kicks the ball so it rolls out in front of the player, who then runs up and shoots the ball. This play can also be done on a direct free kick.

A free kick, especially one near the other team's goal, is always a scoring opportunity. Surprise is most important, and practice can help your team score goals.

Strategy

It is important to practice different plays to use on free kicks from different areas of the field. When the other team has a direct free kick near your goal, four or five of your teammates should stand side by side like a wall, facing the ball and about 10 yards away from the ball. This wall should stand between the ball and the goal, with the end man between the ball and one post. This is to block part of the goal.

The goalie will position himself in the part of the goal that isn't blocked by the wall, to cover that area. The midfielders who are not in the wall should cover the other team's players. This strategy doesn't leave very many places at which the other team can shoot.

When your team has a direct free kick near the other team's goal, the other team will probably set up their defense in the same way. If you want to shoot the ball for a goal, you can chip it (see p. 34) over the wall, to the part of the goal that the goalie isn't covering.

The chip shot is very hard to do. So your team might want to try a different play to deceive the other team. One play is to have three players act as if they're all going to take the shot. The first player runs up to the ball, runs over it and to the side. The second player does the same. The third player starts to run while the second player is still running. He then runs up and shoots the ball. This play should be done quickly so it doesn't give the other team time to think. The ball should be shot into the very corner of the goal the goalie is trying to block.

After you do this play once, the next time you can let the second player or even the first player shoot the ball. If you line up with three players, the other team won't know when to expect the kick.

Another play is to pass the ball to the side of the wall and then shoot. Or shoot hard at the wall. You can make up your own plays or do variations on any of these plays.

PENALTY KICKS

The penalty kick is one of the most dramatic single moments in soccer. A penalty kick is a free shot at the goal with nobody to beat but the goalie. If it is shot correctly, it should be an automatic goal every time.

A penalty kick is awarded if the defending team intentionally commits a foul in their own penalty box. These fouls are kicking, tripping, jumping at an opponent, charging from behind, charging violently, hitting, holding, pushing, or if a player, other than the goalie, hands the ball.

If the referee sees one of these fouls committed in the penalty box, he will blow his whistle and point to the penalty spot, awarding a penalty kick. The ball is set on the penalty spot, 12 yards away from the goal line. All the players, except the kicker and the defending goalie, have to be outside of the penalty box and outside the penalty arc. The players outside of the penalty box will be ready to rush in as soon as the ball is kicked to get a rebound. The goalie has to have both feet touching the goal line.

If you are taking a penalty kick, the first thing you should do is forget about the yelling spectators. Take your mind off the kick until you are ready to take it. If you think of all the spectators yelling, you will get very nervous. If you start thinking about what will happen if you miss, you probably will miss. Just imagine that you have a teammate in the corner of the goal behind the net. Then try to pass the ball right to him.

If the referee puts the ball in a hole or in a place that you don't like, you can move it a couple of inches to the side to a better spot. Brush away any small pebbles that might affect your shot.

Decide where you are going to kick the ball. After you make this decision, keep it. Don't change your mind. If you change your mind when you are about to kick, you will most likely make a bad kick.

The best way to shoot a penalty kick is with the inside of your foot. The kick doesn't have to have tremendous force, as long as it's accurate.

When you practice penalty kicks, practice kicking

different ways. Feel which way is most comfortable. When you find out which way is most comfortable to you, stick to that one way when you practice and in games. When you get really good at penalty kicks, practice shooting for either corner, and with either foot. But in a game only do what you are best at.

Scoring On Penalty Kicks

• When the referee blows his whistle and you are ready to run up to shoot, just look at the ball. Know where you're going to put it. Don't look up at the goalie because he might be leaning to one side to try and make you change your mind.

• When you are running to kick the ball, run normally as you would if you were passing the ball to a teammate. If you run one way then another way to try and fake out the goalie, you will most likely fake yourself out and miss the shot.

• When you shoot, try to get the ball in the lower corner of the goal. If you just kick it as hard as you can to the center of the goal, the goalie will probably save it every time. Try to shoot the ball within 5 feet of either post.

• When you take a penalty kick, wait for the referee to blow his whistle. If the goalie moves before you kick, and you miss, you get another penalty kick. If you score when the goalie moves too soon, it is still a goal. If one of the other team's players jumps into the penalty box before you shoot and you miss, you get the kick over. If you make it, it is still a goal. But if one of your teammates jumps into the penalty box before you shoot and you miss, you miss. And if you score, you have to take the kick over.

• If the ball hits the goalpost and bounces back, and the goalie doesn't touch it, you can't kick the ball again until one of your teammates or a player from the other team touches it first. If you touch the ball, the other team gets a free kick.

• If you shoot and the ball bounces off the goalie, you can shoot again right away.

TACTICS FOR TEAMWORK

WORKING AS A TEAM

In order for your team to work well together, each player must feel good about himself as an individual. The players also have to feel good about each other and about the team as a whole. You can't have any stars or glory hogs on the team, and everyone on the team has to be in good shape and be able to run constantly for the whole game.

If a team works well together, then when a player gets the ball, he knows that the rest of his team will be moving into open space to help him move the ball down the field. He also knows that there are other players who will be backing him up so he doesn't have to worry as much about losing the ball.

When a player on your team gets the ball, think about what you should do. Should you move to the touchline to spread out the defense? Should you break forward? Should you move to open space where your teammate can easily pass the ball to you? You have to use your own good judgment.

Look at the situation, read the play, and see what is needed of you. If you are in a tight area, it might be helpful if you run down the field and take an opponent with you, so your teammate has more space to play the ball. If your teammate has one or two opponents to beat, then you might run toward him, into an open space, where he can pass the ball to you.

You have to practice moving into open space. You have to practice covering for other people. You have to constantly work at reading the plays so it becomes habit. When these decisions become instinctive, you will find that you will be an improved player and that your team will be working well together and winning games.

On the field there are three possible situations: your team has possession of the ball; the other team has possession of the ball; or the ball is being fought over. In each of these cases, you must constantly think: *Where should I go? What should I do?*

GENERAL IDEAS ON TACTICS

As your team gains experience playing together, ideas on tactics will develop. At first your team should try simple moves to get past the other team. If a play works, you should keep practicing it and use it in games.

For example, if one of your midfielders has the ball on one side of the field, the players on the other team will move toward that side of the field. Your midfielder can pass to another midfielder or a winger on the other side of the field with an open area ahead of him. The opposing team will now have to shift to the other side of the field to cover your attack.

Another tactic: A winger has the ball. An inside forward runs down the wing. As soon as he starts running the winger passes the ball down the wing to the open space and runs into the middle to take the inside forward's spot. The inside forward will be running toward that open space to receive the ball. He should have an open field ahead. The inside forwards can also do this play in the middle of the field near the goal. As soon as the pass is received, a shot on goal can be taken.

USING TRIANGLES

A triangle means there are always two players in position near the person with the ball so he can pass it to one of them. Your team should always run and pass in triangles. You can work the ball up the field with triangles. When the ball is passed, a new triangle should be formed with the new person carrying the ball.

The triangle is formed with two players in front and a backup man. This man is known as the *support man*. If an opponent gets the ball from one of the front

support
Man

players, there is a man in back to stop him.

You should generally pass forward. The two front men can work forward with the ball, and if they get into trouble or are covered, then they can pass back to their support. If the two men are in back passing the ball to each other and there is no one backing them up, their pass could be intercepted. The other team could get a breakaway.

When a ball is passed back to the support man, there should be a player next to him to pass to, and a support player in back of him.

Triangles can be used on defense. If the defenders line up in a straight line, a pass can go past all of them and they are all beaten. If one defender backs up the others, even if a pass goes through two of them, the backup player can get it. As soon as the two men in a triangle are beaten, they must hustle to back up the support man.

USING THE WHOLE FIELD

When playing, use the whole width of the field. The two wings should be close to the sidelines. This will force the other team's defense to spread out. When you spread the defense out, you are making it easier for your team, since there are bigger holes to go through.

Your team should pass the ball up the field near the

sidelines. Your midfielders should be running down the middle of the field. When you get down toward the other team's goal, the wing should cross the ball toward the center to a teammate. Then there should be only one or two opponents in the middle of the field with three of your teammates. This would be an easy time to score.

THROUGH PASS

A through pass is both a pass and a play. It is usually used near the goal mouth when your team is trying to score. It is used by either your defenders or your forwards to get the ball through a hole in the defense and into shooting position for a forward who will be running on to the ball.

When you are dribbling the ball and you see one of your forwards to the side of you near an opposing player, this is a perfect time to use a through pass. There is probably going to be a midfielder covering you. Your teammate should run forward between the two opponents. As he starts running, pass the ball forward, between your opponents, so it goes in front of your forward, between him and the goal. Make the pass so that your forward has to take only a few steps up to the ball. Then he can shoot while the opponents are still behind him.

This is a very effective play and can result in many scoring opportunities. But it is hard to get the timing right on this play. You must practice this over and over until you get the timing down correctly.

Practice this play with a friend. Have him run, starting from about the edge of the penalty box, toward the penalty spot in front of the goal. Dribble the ball toward him, to about 10 yards from the edge of the penalty area. As soon as he starts running, pass the ball in front of him so that he can control it and shoot. Keep practicing this move until you get good at it. Later you can get two more people to act as defenders.

MOVING OFF THE BALL

Moving off the ball means moving into position when you do not have the ball to create plays or chances to score. You can either move into position to receive a pass, or take one of your opponents with you so that your teammate with the ball can make a more effective pass. Moving off the ball is very important if your team is to become a better attacking unit.

If a teammate has the ball and you're covered, run quickly to the side, where you may get open for a pass. If the opponent who is guarding you follows you, another teammate might run into your original spot to receive a pass. Or the player with the ball can dribble through the hole you have created. By moving quickly, you may open up a hole for the ball to be passed to a teammate who is open and closer to the goal.

LOSING THE BALL

When your team loses the ball, everyone must hustle to defend. When you lose the ball, immediately chase the man with the ball. If you don't regain possession, you will at least make him rush a pass or maybe lose control of the ball so a teammate can pick it up.

If a passed ball is intercepted by a player on the other team, your teammate nearest to him should immediately chase him to block any pass he might make. This will delay the other team's attack and give the rest of your team time to get back in position to defend.

Always guard an opponent so you are between him and your goal. Every member of your team should be aware of the space between himself and your goal, and every other member of your team. The nearer the attackers come to your goal, the closer they must be guarded.

When your opponents have the ball, there should be more of your players between the ball and your goal than there are opponents.

OTHER IDEAS ON MOVING

When your team has the ball, there should be more teammates near the ball to receive a pass than there are opponents. There should always be a spare man open to get a pass to.

You must develop the spirit and stamina to run into position even if the ball doesn't immediately come your way. Be eager to play the ball and help your teammates. This is pretty much what's called team spirit.

When playing on defense, position yourself so that your opponent with the ball has to dribble around you before he can run for a goal. If you are an outside defender marking a wing, try to keep him on the outside, near the touchline. If he tries to dribble around you, make him dribble toward the outside of the field.

When your team has the ball on the opposite side of the field, drop into the middle of the field to cover the space, but keep your eye on the player you are assigned to cover.

As soon as an opponent with the ball beats you, someone else should cover for you while you quickly run back and cover for him.

DEFENSE IDEAS

When your team is on defense, you must cover for each other, and restrict the amount of time and space the other team has to work in.

• As soon as the other team gets the ball, your team must make it hard for them to do anything. When the opposing goalie gets the ball, your forwards should guard all the opposing defenders tightly. Your midfielders should guard all the other players in the middle of the field, but not necessarily as tightly.

If a defender you are covering receives the ball, quickly hassle him and try to make him rush his play. You must try to block or stop any possible through pass as your opponents move down the field.

When your opponents have the ball in the midfield, your midfield line can retreat toward your goal just enough to make a through pass difficult. If the opponents do make a through pass, one of your midfielders can try to intercept the ball, or your whole team can quickly retreat again. Your midfielders then cover their forwards and your defenders cover the space behind your midfielders. This will take away all the effectiveness of the pass, and your opponents will still have many barriers to pass through.

- As a defender, when the opposing attackers get near, you should mark them more tightly and limit the space in which they can maneuver toward the goal.

- When a player on your team is beaten, your whole defense should shift to cover for him. Then he should run back to cover the space that has been left open, or run into position to back up the rest of your defense.

- If you are a midfielder or a defender guarding an opposing player, and you are the nearest player on your team to another opposing player who has just beaten one of your teammates, then you must leave the player you are covering to pick up the one with the ball. The teammate nearest to you will then pick up your player, and your beaten teammate will cover for him.

IDEAS FOR DEFENDERS

When you are playing defender, work together with the other defenders to stop the opposing forwards. When an opposing player has the ball near you, get in front of him to stop him from breaking toward your goal. Don't get so close to him that he can trick you and beat you. Try to force him to the outside and away from your goal. If he passes to another player near a teammate, your teammate should go out to meet him, just as you did. You leave your opponent a bit open and drop back to cover the space where the opposing player could make a through pass. If the ball is passed back to your opponent, go forward to meet him again, and your teammate should drop back to cover the space.

If you are the only defender near two opposing players, stay back and between them. Stop the player with the ball from dribbling toward your goal by staying in front of him. Stop him from passing by being slightly toward the side where he'll make his pass. If he does pass, then quickly drop back to cover the receiver and use the same tactic.

You must do this until you get help from your teammates. If you're the only defender, and if the other team makes a bad pass, don't go for it unless you're absolutely sure you can get it. If you miss, then they'll beat you. That is especially bad if the play is near your goal and they can score. Just hold them until your teammates recover.

FAIR PLAY

WHAT TO DO WHEN THERE'S A GLORY HOG ON YOUR TEAM

Lots of teams have at least one glory hog. A glory hog isn't very much fun to have on a team. He wrecks team spirit and ruins team play.

Passing is the key to good team play and to scoring

goals. One thing a glory hog won't do is pass the ball. When the hog has possession of the ball, he dribbles too much. Even if he is a good dribbler, there is no way he can dribble through all of the other team's players. Most of the time the hog will lose the ball. When the other team spots a ball hog, they'll double-team him, that is, have two of their players attack him at the same time as soon as he gets the ball.

Another thing a glory hog will do is take lots and lots of bad shots at the goal. Every time he does he loses a chance for his team to score.

Sometimes it's hard to know whether a player is a glory hog or if he just doesn't play well under pressure. A poor player will often take shots at the goal when he should cross the ball to an open teammate.

One way of dealing with a glory hog is to get even with him by not passing the ball to him. However, trying to get even soon wrecks team play. A better way is to talk to the player or ask the coach to talk to him.

During practice, play a small soccer game in which everyone may only touch the ball twice before they must pass it. Each team must pass the ball five times in a row before they can shoot. If this doesn't work, forget about the glory hog. Play the way you should.

HOW TO PLAY AGAINST
SOMEONE TWICE YOUR SIZE

When you start out playing soccer, most of the guys you play against will be bigger than you. Nearly everyone we play against is bigger than we are. So we learned some tips which we can pass along to you.

When you are defending against big players, just get in the way of the one who has the ball. He'll either have to slow down or change his direction. This makes it harder for him to control the ball and easier for your teammates to get the ball away from him.

When he's dribbling, you should shoulder charge him (your shoulder may be against his side) and try to push him off the ball. If he's trying to keep control of the ball, and you are pushing against him, it is tough for him to keep his balance and also keep his mind on what he's doing. If you keep this up, you will throw him off his game. He may start making mistakes.

Practice one-on-one drills with your teammates. Pretty soon you'll find yourself getting the ball away from them a fair number of times. This will build your confidence.

If you're playing man-for-man on one of the other team's stars, stay close to him and get to the passes before he does. If he gets the ball, then you and another player on your team should try to take it away from him at the same time. If he has to watch out for both of you, he'll probably lose the ball or at least kick it badly.

WHEN THE OTHER GUY
PLAYS DIRTY

Sooner or later, when you play soccer, you'll run into someone who plays dirty. He might trip you, push you, kick your shins, or use his elbow and fist. He will usually try this in the middle of the field when the referee isn't looking. He'll try it because most referees will be watching the play and not him. Even if the referee does see the foul, it won't hurt the other team too much because all you'll get is a direct free kick from the middle of the field.

There really aren't too many things you can do about a dirty player except stay away from him and play your own game. You could ask the referee to watch for that

player. If the referee calls enough fouls on him, maybe his team will get on him to stop.

One thing that might help is to wear shin guards. We wore shin guards when we first started playing. Then when we got older, we stopped wearing them because one of our coaches thought they slowed us down. And they were uncomfortable. Now we wear them when we think the other team is going to be rough. We find that wearing shin guards is less uncomfortable than getting a really good kick in the shins. We feel it is better to be safe than sorry!

GO OUT THERE AND HAVE FUN!

Now that you know the game, join a soccer team. Go out there and have fun.

Practice regularly. Several short practices each week are better than one long, tiring practice. As you practice, invent games and contests for yourself. Keep practicing your skills even when it seems hopeless, and you feel you'll never master them. With time, it will all come together.

If you keep playing, unimportant things such as your team's standing will fade from your mind. A year later you probably won't remember the number of games you won or lost. But you will remember whether or not you had a good time.

When you mess up (and everyone messes up sometime), don't worry! Soccer is a fast game and no one remembers individual plays for very long. If you start to worry about what you did wrong on the last play your mind will be off the game, and you'll mess up on the next play.

Don't let the spectators distract you. Don't argue with the other team, the officials, or with your own teammates. Don't compare yourself to others. Set your own goals, and measure your progress against your own goals. Make one of your most important goals keeping in good shape. You'll feel and look better. If you keep in shape, you should consider that alone a major accomplishment. The team that is in better condition will score the most goals, especially toward the end of the game.

Spirit and determination are often more important than skills. Cheer your teammates on and your team will be more fun to be with, and will most likely play better. Remember, soccer is just a game. And there is always your next game and your next season to look forward to.

WORDS YOU SHOULD KNOW

arc–The quarter circle at each corner of the field in which the ball is placed for a corner kick.

attacker–A player trying to score during a game.

breakaway–When a player has the ball and is past all his opponents and has an open field on which to dribble between him and the goal.

call–Shouting to a teammate to let him know where you are so he can pass the ball to you. Also a decision made by a referee.

centering–Kicking the ball from one of the wings into the goal area or penalty area.

charging–(See **shoulder charge.**)

chip–Causing the ball to travel in the air by kicking underneath it.

chip pass–A short kick over an opponent's head to a teammate.

chip shot–A kick at goal lifted usually over an opposing defender's or goalie's head.

corner flag–The flag on a pole at each corner of the field. They help the referee see if the ball crosses the goal line or the touchline.

corner kick–A kick taken from the arc at the corner of the field by the attacking team when the defending team last touched the ball before it crossed the goal line.

cover (or **mark**)–Guarding a player on the other team to stop him from getting the ball.

crossbar–The top bar of the goal which is parallel to the ground.

dangerous play–Any play, movement, or action that puts an opponent, a teammate, or yourself in a position where you may get injured.

defender–Sometimes called fullback. The players who are mainly responsible for stopping the opposing team from scoring.

defense–The part of your team that tries to stop the other team from scoring.

dribbling–Moving the ball with the foot with successive kicks.

far post–The goalpost that is farthest away from where the ball is.

forwards–The players who take most of the shots and do most of the scoring.

foul–An illegal play or movement by a player.

free kick–A kick given to a team when the other team commits a foul. The ball is placed on the ground where the foul occurred. All the players on the other team must remain at least 10 yards away from the ball until it is kicked and travels its circumference.

goal–When the ball goes between the goalposts, under the crossbar, and over the goal line to score a point.

goal (or goalie) box–The area in which the ball is placed to take a goal kick. Also called goal, or goalie, area.

goalie–The one player on your team who is allowed to touch the ball with his hands in the penalty area. His job is to stop the ball from going into the goal, and then to get the ball to a teammate to start play again.

goal kick–A free kick taken by the defending team when the attacking team kicks the ball out of bounds across the goal line.

goal line–The boundary line on which the goalposts stand across each end of the field.

goalmouth–The area immediately in front of the goal.

goalposts–The posts that hold up the crossbar. Also called uprights.

half-line–The line across the middle of the field which divides the field in half. Also called halfway line.

halftime–A game is divided into two equally timed halves. After the first half is up, a short break is taken and the teams switch sides of the field and the goal they are defending.

half volley–A ball kicked as soon as it starts rising from a bounce.

hand ball–Touching the ball with your hands or arms. It's only legal for the goalie within the penalty box.

heading–Moving the ball by hitting it with the fore-head.

instep drive–A kick or shot taken with the part of the foot covered by your shoelaces.

linesman–An official near one of the touchlines who waves his flag to signal to the referee when the ball is out of bounds or a player is offside.

marking–(See **cover.**)

midfielder–Sometimes called halfback. The players who play around the middle of the field.

near post–The goalpost nearest the ball.

net–The openwork plastic or string that is tied to the goalposts to catch the ball. It makes it easier to tell when a goal is scored.

offense–The part of a team trying to score.

opponent–The person or persons on the other team in a game.

off-the-ball–Running without the ball to move into an open space so you can receive a pass or help a teammate receive a pass.

offside–Being ahead of the ball when it is played in your direction. In order to be called offside, you must be in your opponent's half of the field and have fewer than two opponents ahead of you when the ball is played to you by a teammate.

pass–Using any part of your body except your hands or arms to hit the ball to a teammate.

penalty arc–The semicircle at the top of the penalty box. It is 10 yards from the penalty spot. Neither team can be inside the arc when a penalty kick is being taken.

penalty box–The lines that form the rectangle within which the goalie may use his hands to touch the ball. It's the second rectangle in front of the goal.

penalty kick–A free kick on goal inside the penalty area with only the goalie to beat. It is given after the defense has committed a foul inside the penalty box.

penalty spot–The spot in the center of the penalty box, 12 yards away from the goal line.

power kick–A hard, fast shot or kick.

referee–The person who controls the soccer game.

restarts–The process of starting play again after a goal, or after the ball has gone out of bounds.

screening–Keeping your body between the ball and the person trying to take it away from you when you are dribbling.

shot–An attempt to score a goal.

shoulder charge–Using your shoulder by leaning against the shoulder of an opponent to push him off balance so you can gain possession of the ball. The ball must be within 3 or 4 feet of you or this charging is illegal.

slide tackle–Gaining possession of the ball by kicking it away from your opponent's feet while you are sliding on the ground.

strikers–The forwards in the middle of the forward line.

sweeper–The sweeper is a defender who doesn't have a special player to mark and usually plays behind the other defenders to back them up.

tackling–Using the feet to take the ball away from an opposing player.

tactics–Strategy used to out-play the other team.

throw-in–When the ball goes out of bounds across the touchline, the ball is put back into play with a throw-in. A throw-in is made by holding the ball with both hands behind the head. Then the hands are brought forward to throw the ball.

touchline–The lines on the long side of the field which indicate the boundaries.

trapping–Gaining control of a moving ball by stopping it with a part of the body.

tripping–Causing an opponent to fall by hitting his feet out from beneath him.

volley–Kicking the ball while it is in the air.

wing–The parts of the field toward the touchlines. Also the forward who plays on that part of the field.